Hand and Foot

Sally Prue

Illustrated by **Alex Paterson**

OXFORD
UNIVERSITY PRESS

Letter from the Author

There are bits of stories to be found all over the place. To make a book, they need to be arranged, of course, but that's the fun of it.

Where did I find the story for *Hand and Foot*? Well, the 1790s, when the book is set, was a time of astonishing change. People were quickly becoming desperately poor or very rich; there were new laws and new technology, great heroes and dastardly villains (and very few drains). A search through some portraits of the period inspired the character of the shy but rich Marianne, as well as a thoroughly nasty governess and a cheerful orphan called Gravity (as an adopted child I often find myself writing about orphans).

Above all, I discovered that although in those days everything was different, everything was also the same: bad people needed to be faced with courage, and good ones rewarded.

That's Gravity and Marianne's story, and it's mine. And of course it's yours, too.

Sally Prue

Chapter 1
The Force of Gravity

'I wish I could go to school,' said Marianne, wistfully.

Her brother Lawrence's bed was stacked with neatly folded clothes – shirts, neck-cloths and stockings – that Marianne had spent the summer making and mending. Tomorrow Lawrence was leaving for school in London, and he wouldn't be back until nearly Christmas.

'We could swap places, if you like,' Lawrence suggested. This was Lawrence's first term at boarding school, and he wasn't at all sure he'd like it. 'Probably no one would notice the difference.'

Marianne laughed. People did say that she and Lawrence were alike – they both had the same wavy fair hair – but she was a year younger than Lawrence and not nearly as tall.

And, of course, she was a girl.

'I'd love to go to London to see old King George and all the princesses,' she said. 'And it'd probably do you good to have lessons with Miss Dobbs. She'd teach you to be quiet and useful and polite.'

'Miss Dobbs couldn't teach *anyone* to be polite,' replied Lawrence, scornfully. 'She's always rude to everybody!'

There was a tremendous bumping and clattering and puffing outside the room, as if someone was chasing a bull up the stairs, and then something hit the door with such a great thump that it burst open and revealed a girl of about Marianne's age staggering around under the weight of a leather-bound trunk.

The girl let the trunk drop on to the floorboards with a crash that echoed round the room. Wisps of black hair were escaping from under her servant's cap, and there were streaks of rust from the nails on the trunk all down her apron.

'Well, I don't know how we're going to get that trunk downstairs again when it's full,' the girl announced. 'It's already stretched my arms as long as an organ grinder's monkey's!'

This was the new chambermaid. She was called Gravity Sparrow, but there was nothing the least bit grave or sparrow-like about her. She was sturdy, cheerful, and much too loud and chatty.

Gravity Sparrow leaned against the door frame to get her breath back.

'We'll have to ride the trunk downstairs like a sledge,' suggested Lawrence, grinning at her. Gravity had often worked in the vegetable garden until her recent promotion to chambermaid. This meant that she and Lawrence had spent a lot of time getting happily grubby together, and they were great friends.

5

Marianne, on the other hand, hardly knew Gravity Sparrow at all. Her governess, Miss Dobbs, didn't allow Marianne to go beyond the flower gardens.

Gravity (*never* was there such a badly-named girl) threw back her head and laughed loudly.

'Ride it down the stairs?' she said. 'That'd make a fine racket! It'd most likely break half our bones too!'

'Well, it wouldn't be the first disaster we've had together,' said Lawrence, grinning, and Gravity laughed some more.

Marianne felt a twinge of annoyance. She'd wanted Lawrence all to herself on this last afternoon, and here was silly Gravity Sparrow, who was just a maid, barging in and taking over.

'That would be very foolish,' she said, severely.

Gravity's face fell, which wasn't surprising because Marianne had sounded nearly as snappish as Miss Dobbs.

'I wouldn't really—' Gravity began, anxiously, but Lawrence got up.

'I'll come downstairs with you, Gravity,' he said. 'I need to say goodbye to the horses.'

They went off together and Marianne was left alone.

Stupid Gravity, Marianne thought, angry and regretful, as their footsteps clattered away down the stairs.

* * *

'Gravity does her best, you know,' said Lawrence to Marianne, later, as he made his farewell tour of the house. 'Mama and Papa find her very amusing. That time she managed to let the goat loose in the parlour when Sir William and his sister were visiting—'

'That was very distressing to Miss Dobbs,' said Marianne, feeling cross again.

'Yes, it was, wasn't it,' said Lawrence, happily. 'The way the old girl screamed and jumped about!'

Marianne said nothing. It *had* been funny, but it still wasn't fair. Why did everyone make such a fuss of Gravity Sparrow when she was so silly – and in front of guests, too? Sir William Spence was, admittedly, quite foolish himself, but then Sir William owned most of the district and so he was important. Mama and Papa kept hoping Sir William would get cleverer as he got older, but in the meantime they asked him to dinner very often so they could hear all about his estate and drop helpful hints. Sometimes it seemed to Marianne that the more trouble you caused the more notice people took of you. It was hard when you were trying your best to be good and quiet and obedient.

Marianne felt almost glad for a moment that Mama and Papa were going away. They were taking Lawrence to school in the carriage, and then they were going on to make a tour of the new northern factories. That meant Miss Dobbs would be in charge of the house for the next couple of months.

Marianne didn't like her governess very much, but at least Miss Dobbs valued good behaviour when she saw it.

* * *

The early-morning bustle of the goodbyes was over and the carriage carrying Mama and Papa and Lawrence had turned the corner and trundled out of sight. Marianne stopped waving her handkerchief and used it to dry her eyes.

She heard a flapping above her. Gravity Sparrow was leaning out of an attic window, waving a duster like mad. Gravity must still be able to see the carriage from up there.

Marianne made her way sadly up to the schoolroom.

'Today you shall learn the major Roman Emperors,' said Miss Dobbs, as stiff and straight inside her shawl as if she had a broomstick for a spine. 'And if you know them off by heart by breakfast time, Marianne, then you may look at my locket that was given to me by my brother the judge.'

Augustus. Tiberius. Caligula ...

(Where were Lawrence and Mama and Papa now? They must have reached the London road.)

... Pertinax. Julianus. Severus.

And that was the end of those wretched emperors at last.

Miss Dobbs's locket contained a portrait of the stout woman who had been her aunt. She had been as bulgy and greasy as her niece was thin and dry, but Marianne liked the tiny pearls set around the frame and the little dog nestled in the folds of the woman's shiny dress.

9

'I wish Mama might bring me a ribbon of the same pink as your aunt's dress, Miss Dobbs.'

'You should not be vain, child,' said Miss Dobbs, holding out a thin hand for the locket. 'Now,' she went on, with a disapproving flick of her shawl's spider-leg fringe, 'you may fill your inkwell. I have some proverbs for you to copy.'

Marianne sighed. Mama would be sure to bring her a present, all the same. There were wonderful things being made in the new factories in the north. Why, Papa said that soon all the poor people would move away to work in them and that Sir William Spence would have no workers left to farm his estate. Sir William had shaken his foolish head at this, but admitted that his estate was bringing in much less money than it should.

'It's a good job I have my steward,' Sir William had told them. 'A wonderful man: couldn't manage without him. Fond of my sister. He has a very rich old uncle, you know.'

His sister, Miss Spence, had looked uneasy, but had said nothing.

Marianne was filling her inkwell carefully when there was a jumbled clumping on the stairs. Before Marianne had time to move, the schoolroom door had burst open, hitting her elbow, and a long loop of black ink had shot out of the big ink bottle and splashed itself across Miss Dobbs's shawl.

'Breakfast's all ready,' announced Gravity Sparrow, cheerfully. 'But do you want it served in the – *oh no!*'

Miss Dobbs turned on Gravity, her bony face ugly with rage.

'Look what you've done! Wretched girl! Quick, quick, out of the way, you great lout – I must attend to this at once or my shawl will be ruined. Marianne, leave that and come along – I shall need help. Out of my way, I say, you clumsy oaf! Quick, child, quick, before it dries!'

Miss Dobbs pushed her way past Gravity, all fury and flying fringe, and Marianne hurried along the corridor after her. Poor Gravity was going to be in terrible trouble, but Marianne was secretly just a little glad that here, at last, was someone who didn't think Gravity Sparrow was utterly charming and wonderful, whatever she did.

'Bungling, awkward creature,' muttered Miss Dobbs, in her narrow bedroom, rubbing at her soiled shawl with some stuff that stank of smelling salts. 'I always said that it was a great mistake to take an orphan into the house. My brother the judge would never have dreamed of doing such a thing. But of course your mother is kindness itself.'

Marianne gave Miss Dobbs a fresh piece of cotton soaked in the sour-smelling ammonia. The stain was coming out quite nicely. Luckily the ink hadn't touched the fringe.

'I shall give orders for Gravity Sparrow to be confined to the servants' basement until further notice,' went on Miss Dobbs, dabbing viciously. 'She may be of some use scrubbing turnips or fetching coal, but she is plainly not fit to wait on respectable people. And I'm sure that if your dear mother were here she'd agree with me.'

Mama would have done nothing of the kind. If Mama had been at home she'd have laughed, given Miss Dobbs a new shawl and given Gravity some how-to-open-a-door lessons.

But again Marianne was quiet and good and said nothing.

* * *

Susannah Coker answered the schoolroom bell for the rest of that day. Susannah was an excellent servant. She opened doors quietly, bobbed respectful curtseys, and apart from her face (which was generally scrunched up with bad temper) she always looked freshly ironed.

Now that Lawrence's shirts were finished, Marianne was making a grey cloak for a poor person, and it was just when she was putting away her sewing at the end of the day that the real trouble started.

'I cannot find my locket that my brother the judge gave me,' Miss Dobbs said irritably, fussing through the thimbles and threads in her needlework box. 'Surely I put it back safely this morning, but it's not here. You did give it back to me, Marianne?'

'Oh yes,' said Marianne. 'Do you remember, Miss Dobbs, you asked for it back when I wished for a ribbon as pink as your aunt's dress?'

'So I did,' agreed Miss Dobbs. 'Then it certainly must be here, for I haven't taken my bag from the room. It must have fallen out when I took out my handkerchief.'

Marianne got down on the floor and looked along the shiny floorboards. The afternoon was gloomy, so Miss Dobbs lit a candle and passed it to her so she could see into the corners.

'Take care, child, or you'll set your hair on fire. This silly fashion for having one's hair dangling everywhere is *most* dangerous. Can you see it?'

There wasn't much furniture in the schoolroom: only two desks, two chairs, a pile of sewing boxes and a bookcase filled with sermons, arithmetic books and improving fables in English and French. Marianne and Miss Dobbs moved everything, but there was no sign of the locket.

'But where can it have gone?' asked Miss Dobbs. 'It was here this morning, and no one would have come up here since then – '

Miss Dobbs's long face was suddenly overtaken by a look of horrid revelation.

'Gravity Sparrow,' she said.

Marianne sat up from where she was searching the dusty floor under the bookcase yet again.

'Gravity? But surely Gravity wouldn't—'

Miss Dobbs clasped her hands together as if she were praying for something very serious.

'We left her here alone after she threw the ink on me,' she said. 'She must have done the whole thing on purpose to steal the locket. It is the only possibility.'

Again Marianne said nothing, even though Gravity hadn't actually thrown ink on anybody.

'I am very much afraid,' said Miss Dobbs, red spots appearing high on her cheeks, 'that Gravity Sparrow is a *thief*!'

Chapter 2
A Sparrow Falls

The schoolroom bell rang in the basement just as the servants were drinking their tea.

'Blow it!' said Susannah Coker, crossly. 'What's old Dobbs doing up in the schoolroom at this hour?'

'Well, never mind,' said Mrs Bateman the housekeeper. 'It won't take you long to nip up and sort her out. I'll put the saucer over your tea to keep it warm.'

'*You* should be doing this, Gravity,' said Susannah, angrily, as she put down her tea. Susannah was always angry: she started the day being angry about having to get up and finished it being angry about having to go to bed. 'If I get stomach ache with running about before my dinner's settled it'll be all down to your clumsiness, Gravity Sparrow!'

'I'll polish the brass for you to make up for it,' offered Gravity, but Susannah only snorted and flounced out.

'Now, don't you worry about Susannah, Gravity,' Mrs Bateman said firmly. 'There won't be much to do upstairs now the master and mistress and Master Lawrence are away. Susannah can easily manage by herself, for all her moaning. Anyway, this will give us a chance to train you up properly. Why, by the time the mistress comes home again you'll be so trim and quick-fingered she'll hardly know you.'

Gravity smiled, much comforted. She'd been rather sorrowful at being banished to the basement, but she was discovering that in some ways it was more fun being down here with the others than tiptoeing about up in the grand family rooms.

Joseph the footman had stretched out his long legs towards the grate. 'I just hope Miss Dobbs isn't going to expect us to wait on her hand and foot,' he said. 'I was looking forward to a bit of a holiday.'

Mrs Bateman snorted. 'Miss Dobbs? Let her try it, that's all. She's only the governess, when all's said and done. The mistress, she said to me, "Miss Dobbs is in my place upstairs, but you're the one who knows how the house works, so you must up and tell her if anything is needed, just like you tell me."'

'Tell her we need a proper lady in charge of the house,' said Joseph, with a snort. 'And not some dragon that's never learned any manners!'

Gravity was still laughing at this when Susannah came back down the basement stairs.

For once Susannah didn't look cross. If anything she looked frightened. She was nearly as pale as her cap.

'What's the matter?' demanded Mrs Bateman, alarmed. 'There's no one been taken ill?'

Susannah tottered forward and clutched at the back of Joseph's chair.

'It's Miss Dobbs,' she said weakly.

'Dead?' gasped Joseph, between horror and a certain degree of hope.

'No,' said Susannah. 'But she says … she says to send Joseph for the constable!'

There was a moment's silence. The constable was the old man you paid if you wanted to have someone arrested for doing a crime.

'The constable?' echoed Mrs Bateman, bewildered. 'The constable, come to this house? And why should a constable be needed here, pray?'

Susannah burst into tears.

'To take Gravity to prison!' she wailed.

* * *

Mrs Bateman hurried Gravity up the stairs to where Miss Dobbs sat in the drawing room, her dress as grey as ice. Her face was icy too: Mrs Bateman's bustling anger seemed to freeze in the air before it could reach her.

'I cannot be responsible for keeping a thief in the house,' Miss Dobbs told Mrs Bateman, stonily.

'But I'm not a thief,' said Gravity, almost in tears. 'I'm not. I never saw the locket. Honestly, Miss Dobbs, I never did!'

Mrs Bateman looked Miss Dobbs straight in the eye.

'And that has the ring of truth, Miss Dobbs, if I know anything about it.'

'Of course it has the ring of truth,' replied Miss Dobbs, irritably. 'The child will have been brought up to lie and steal since she was an infant.'

Mrs Bateman took a hasty step forward.

'Gravity has been brought up in this house since she was seven years old!' she said, angrily. 'And I've never known a more honest girl than Gravity Sparrow. Nor a more willing one, neither!'

'Or one clumsier,' said Miss Dobbs, coldly.

Mrs Bateman stopped for a moment.

'I'm not saying the girl's dainty,' she admitted. 'And she can cause more trouble fetching a splash of milk than anyone could dream of – goats in the parlour, indeed!'

Gravity blushed. She would never forget that goat for as long as she lived.

'But that's not a matter for the constable,' Mrs Bateman went on. 'I'm sorry your locket is lost, Miss Dobbs, but I'm quite sure that Gravity had no hand in the matter.'

Miss Dobbs sat as still as a statue on a tomb.

'Well, we shall find proof of Sparrow's guilt, then,' she said at last. 'Come along, Marianne, your young eyes may be of use. Where does the girl sleep?'

Gravity and Susannah slept in bunk beds in a cupboard in the basement. Everyone watched as Miss Dobbs pulled the bedclothes off both beds, but all she found when she searched through them was a pack of letters tied with a blue ribbon addressed to *Miss Susannah Coker* in one, and a pretty silver button in the other.

'And where did you steal this?' demanded Miss Dobbs, holding it in Gravity's face.

'I didn't steal it, I didn't!' said Gravity, shaking her head so hard her cap nearly fell off.

'Then where would you have got such a thing?'

'I got served it up in my Christmas pudding,' explained Gravity, anxiously. 'And Mrs Bateman said I was lucky, for that meant it was mine. But I would have given it back if anyone had wanted it.'

Mrs Bateman sighed.

'And have you been treasuring that button all these months? Oh, you foolish child!'

Miss Dobbs sniffed.

'The child is plainly a magpie, ready to scoop up anything she sees. My locket has probably already been passed to some accomplice – the grocer's boy, or some other vagrant. Goodness knows how many coins and valuables the wretched child has sold over the years.'

'But I haven't, madam!' exclaimed Gravity. 'I've never stolen anything.'

'Never?' demanded Miss Dobbs.

Gravity thought hard.

'Well ... I might have helped myself to a baby carrot or two, perhaps, when we were thinning them out in the garden.'

'That's not stealing, Gravity,' said Mrs Bateman, between exasperation and affection. 'Miss Dobbs, there's no proof here that Gravity's taken anything.'

Miss Dobbs raised a cold eyebrow.

'Perhaps not,' she said, 'but I must prevent the child stealing any more of the master's property, all the same. If she cannot be turned over to the constable then she must be turned out of the house.'

Gravity looked from Mrs Bateman's shocked face to Marianne's.

'But I live here!' Gravity said.

Miss Dobbs smiled a small, satisfied smile and turned to make her way back up the basement stairs.

'Not any longer,' she said. 'Mrs Bateman, make sure you take back those good new clothes the mistress has been kind enough to give the girl. Oh, and my shawl is in need of a thorough rinsing. See to it.'

* * *

Miss Dobbs left everyone too shocked to move. Even Marianne was too weak at the knees to follow her governess up the stairs.

'But ... where shall I go?' asked Gravity, at last.

Mrs Bateman gathered her wits.

'Don't worry, Gravity,' she said hurriedly. 'You're a strong, healthy girl. I'm sure there'll be plenty of jobs you can turn your hand to.'

'But what about her clothes?' wailed Susannah. 'Her old ones she had in the garden have all been torn up for rags.'

Mrs Bateman shook a fist in the direction of the stairs.

'Wretched woman! To think of dismissing Gravity like that when the poor girl has nowhere to go! Gravity, I have a warm woollen dress you can have. Though it'll be too big for you. Oh dear.'

'There'll be clothes in the poor box,' suggested Joseph. Marianne and Miss Dobbs spent hours every day making clothes for the poor.

Marianne felt even more shocked to think that Gravity was going to be poor, like the grubby and half-starved people she so often saw from the windows of the house.

'That's a good thought,' said Mrs Bateman. 'Susannah, run upstairs and see what you can find. Oh, and bring Miss Dobbs's dirty shawl down while you're about it. We don't want her down here again causing more trouble.'

Susannah came down with a pile of newly-made clothes from which Mrs Bateman chose a shift, an apron, a cap and some petticoats. To these she added her old-fashioned dress and an ancient red cloak that hung by the kitchen door in case anyone needed to go out to the privy in the rain.

Marianne sat on the stairs and watched all this. She was full of doubt. She supposed Gravity Sparrow must have stolen the locket if Miss Dobbs said so, but Gravity looked so awful when she came back from her room dressed in her new clothes. The cloak was grubby, the dress was too big all over, and the cap flopped like a pancake over her eyes.

Susannah snatched up Miss Dobbs's damp shawl in a rage, screwed it into a ball and hurled it into the laundry basket with such force that even the splayed-out spider-leg fringe didn't stop it landing with a small thump.

'And the stupid thing can wait there till spring to be

washed for all I care,' she announced. 'Oh, Mrs Bateman, what's Gravity going to *do*? No one will give her a job as a servant dressed like that.'

Gravity looked round at all the serious faces, and she swallowed. But then she put back her shoulders and stood up tall.

'Gardening,' she said bravely. 'I know all about that. You don't have to be finely dressed for gardening. And I'm not afraid of animals, so I could be a cowherd. Why, I'm not afraid of *anything*!'

Joseph shook his head.

'Sometimes you need to be afraid,' he told her. 'You're going to have to keep your wits about you, Gravity Sparrow.'

Marianne shivered at the thought of being faced with a herd of cows – but then Gravity was only a servant, she told herself. She'd been born in the workhouse in Guildston. For her, hard and dirty work was normal.

Everyone was hugging Gravity, and saying goodbye, and telling her to be good.

At least she'll have the money from selling the locket, thought Marianne to herself, as Gravity took one last look around and then stepped resolutely over the kitchen doorstep. For a moment Marianne saw Gravity briskly climbing the area steps to the street.

And then Gravity Sparrow was gone.

Chapter 3
The Law of the Land

Gravity paused at the top of the area steps to push her cap out of her eyes. It was strange to be out in the street by herself, and even stranger to have nowhere to go.

She looked around briefly and set off in the direction of the town centre, following the way the master's carriage had gone only that morning.

Only that morning: what an age it seemed since she'd waved goodbye to Master Lawrence. What a difference a single day could make!

Gravity stopped at the corner for a last look back at the house. Then she swallowed down the great ball of sadness that had swelled up inside her and walked determinedly round the corner and into the high street.

There were shop windows here displaying hanks of wool, or spectacles, or medicines, and she became so engrossed by one window full of cakes that she had to step smartly out of the way to avoid being run over by a two-wheeled gig. It came along very fast and spattered her cloak as it turned into the stable yard of the inn opposite. This inn had a picture of a man in a crown hanging above the door.

Gravity, curious, crossed the road and peered in through the diamond panes of the windows. There was a fire burning inside even though it was not really cold at all, and there were people sitting chatting to each other. It looked peaceful and friendly.

Gravity sighed and walked on. It would be dark in an hour or so, and she had to find work before then or she'd have to spend the night under a tree.

The road wound down a hill and over a bridge, and after that the countryside began.

There wasn't much traffic. She met a pedlar trudging along under his pack, and then a gentleman on a chestnut horse trotting smartly past a trundling blue cart whose driver seemed to be asleep. Then there was a long gap, and then at last a man pushing a barrow.

The man with the barrow was old and poor, but Gravity curtseyed politely and wished him a good evening.

He grunted a reply, but didn't stop.

'I'm looking for a job,' Gravity said, turning to walk along beside him.

Grunt.

'I've done gardening, mostly, but I'm willing to do anything.'

The old man carried on walking, and Gravity walked with him. It was getting cold now, and the shadows under the trees were vast mouths of darkness.

'I'm quite strong,' Gravity assured him. 'And I'm healthy too. And ... and I've nowhere to go, sir.'

The old man put down the barrow at that and looked Gravity up and down.

'I can't pay you,' he told her, brusquely. 'But if you can get that barrow home then you can stay the night.'

Gravity was so grateful she could have hugged him.

'Oh, I will,' she said. 'Thank you. Thank you kindly, sir.'

The old man grunted and walked on.

By the time the old man turned off the road on to a narrow track, Gravity's hands were sore from the rough handles of the barrow, but she gritted her teeth

and carried on. Dark clouds were coming over, and she definitely wanted a door between her and the night.

'Here we are,' announced the man.

There was a building a little way ahead. Gravity thought it was a stable until the man let out a cry of 'Wife!' and a woman, even tinier and more bent than her husband, appeared at the door.

'Husband?' she asked. 'Who's that you've got with you?'

'Girl looking for work,' said the man.

His wife looked frightened.

'But where will we put her?'

'With the cow, Wife, where do you think?'

The old woman viewed Gravity as if she were a dog that might suddenly decide to bite.

'But what shall she eat?' she asked.

'Same as us,' said the man.

'Well,' said the woman. 'You'd best come in, then.'

* * *

The only thing Gravity had ever owned in her life was the silver button from the Christmas pudding, but she discovered that this couple, the Hodges, were poorer than she had ever been. Their cottage was miserably cold and damp, and their little strip of land only just gave them enough to live on. Gravity was more grateful than ever to be safe and fed.

The next day Mr Hodge found Gravity some digging to do, and the day after that there was a hedge that needed cutting back. Gradually Gravity realized she'd found a new home. She grew quite fond of the Hodges and their warm, sweet-smelling cow, even though the cow kept trying to eat her cap.

'I'm sorry we can't give you money,' explained Mrs Hodge, at the end of Gravity's first week, 'but we're grateful for your help. We can't keep our patch going by ourselves properly, now our son has moved up north.'

Mr Hodge grunted.

'It's very fine in the north, our son says,' went on Mrs Hodge, wistfully. 'All these new factories. Why, they say that even quite young children can earn their living. It's wonderful how they've got things worked out.'

This provoked Mr Hodge into a rare speech.

'Well, we're not going, not even if the streets are paved with bread!' he announced, fiercely. '*This* is my land, as it was my father's and his father's before that. And no one's going to shift me!'

Mrs Hodge blinked her watery blue eyes at him.

'This new law from London will shift you,' she said, but Mr Hodge only snarled and went out.

Mrs Hodge explained it to Gravity later. The lawyers in London had said that everyone's little patches had to be joined together into big ones, and soon Sir William Spence would be turning all the little farmers off their land. The common where the cow grazed was being taken away too.

'Sir William has promised he'll give us work and rent us a brand new cottage but, Mr Hodge, he still doesn't like it. Not that he's got any choice:

'The law locks up the man or woman
Who steals the goose from off the common,
But lets the greater felon loose
Who steals the common off the goose,' she recited, sadly.

31

But the autumn went on and no one bothered the Hodges. In October the pheasants were released from Sir William's rearing pens. They had even less sense than Sir William himself and sometimes flopped down on Mr Hodge's patch, even occasionally dropping dead on it (Gravity never asked any questions about this) and had to be hastily cooked to hide the evidence.

But then one day in December, as Gravity was digging turnips for supper, a group of men came riding up the track to the cottage. She recognized Sir William from her

time at the big house and dropped a curtsey that dunked her skirts even deeper in the mud of the field.

One of Sir William's companions, a handsome, clever-looking person with smooth cheeks, rode forward and read out something from a piece of paper. Gravity didn't understand it, but Mr Hodge scowled and Mrs Hodge began to cry.

'Now, this is for everyone's good,' said Sir William, anxiously. 'Your land belongs to me now, by order of the law, but my steward here will pay you for it. And you won't suffer, for there'll be work for you on my estate, and a house for you too, as promised.'

Mr Hodge snatched the paper the smooth man held out, threw it on the ground and stamped on it. Sir William looked quite alarmed.

'Well, I'll leave you to sort out the details with my steward,' he said hastily, turned his horse, and trotted away.

'I'm not working for Sir William, nor for any man!' declared Mr Hodge.

'Then you'll starve,' said the smooth man, with a shrug.

'Oh no I won't!' replied Mr Hodge, sturdily. 'Wife!'

Mrs Hodge was holding a broom as if she meant to wield it against the lot of them.

'Husband?' she said.

'Pack your bits and bobs. We're moving north.'

Chapter 4
Hasty Pudding

The smooth man waited until Sir William's shiny horse was back on the road, and then he gestured to the men behind him.

They came forward grimly with hammers and axes.

'No!' shouted Gravity, running forward brandishing her garden fork, but the men pushed her away and she fell backwards into the mud.

The men began to pull down the thatch of the cottage.

'Wait, wait!' shouted Mrs Hodge, hobbling into the cottage. But the men didn't wait. Soon the men were pushing the pulled-down thatch against the cottage walls.

'Come out, Wife, come out!' Mr Hodge shouted. 'They're going to set the place ablaze!'

Mrs Hodge appeared in the doorway clutching an ancient bonnet in one hand and a large bundle in the other.

'All right!' Mr Hodge shouted at the steward. 'You give me my money for my house and my cow, and then you can do your filthy work as you please.'

The steward looked puzzled.

'But I've already given you your money,' he told him. 'Haven't I, lads? You saw me do it just now, didn't you?

All those golden guineas I placed in his hand?' The steward laughed cruelly. 'Be off with you, old man. Stand aside!'

Mr Hodge raised a fist, but his wife stepped between them and in the end he only gave a snarl of anger and turned away. Gravity grabbed the barrow and followed them down the track.

The warmth of the great leaping fire beat against her back as she went.

* * *

'That was a good thought, Gravity, to bring the barrow,' said Mrs Hodge as they turned on to the main road. 'That bundle was enough to tear my old arms from their sockets.'

'Shall I run after Sir William and tell him what his steward's done?' asked Gravity, quite breathless with indignation.

Mr Hodge smiled grimly.

'No, child,' he said. 'It'd be our word against the steward's, and that'd be no good. No, we're finished here now. We'll be off north to find our son. He'll be expecting us, for he always said it'd come to this. Wife, you took the iron box from under the mattress?'

'Of course I did,' said Mrs Hodge. 'It's all right, we've got enough money to get us both north, and then our son will take us in till we can find work.'

Gravity wanted to say, *What about me?*

They came at last to the King's Head, which was where the stagecoaches stopped. The yard was busy with carriages and men leading horses.

'Only two days from London to Manchester by stagecoach, nowadays,' said Mr Hodge. 'We'll be with our son soon.'

Mrs Hodge turned to Gravity.

'I'm sorry we can't take you with us, child,' she said. 'But here, my dear, you can have my old hat. I shall wear my bonnet now I'm going to live in a town.'

Gravity had known they wouldn't take her, really. She sighed to herself and tried to look pleased with the hat.

Along the road a horn sounded.

'There's the stagecoach,' said Mr Hodge. 'Quick, Wife, we must buy us some dinner to take along with us.'

Mrs Hodge looked round and saw a girl running out of the inn bearing a tray of pies.

'Can you bring us a couple of those?' she asked the girl. 'We'll be half starved if we have to wait until London to get our dinner.'

The girl was out of breath with hurrying.

'I'll do my best,' she said, 'but we're that short-staffed at the moment, what with the scullery maid having left.'

The great stagecoach drove thunderously into the yard as she spoke, and suddenly everything was happening very fast. Men were running forward to lead the horses away to the stables, and more men were putting fresh horses in their place. And now people were jumping stiffly down from the coach and others were climbing up, some to take places inside the coach itself, and some to claim seats on the roof. There was a great throwing-up of bundles and a handing-up of hot pies and a wrapping-round of shawls.

The big horses were puffing out billows of steam and striking impatient sparks off the cobbles with their iron shoes.

And now, with the horn blowing and the whip cracking, the coach was in motion again, and Gravity was waving and waving as Mr and Mrs Hodge dwindled away into the distance.

When they'd quite gone, Gravity Sparrow discovered that she was being watched. Across the road, staring at her open-mouthed, was a fair-haired girl of about her own age.

Marianne.

Miss Dobbs was there too. Gravity, suddenly aware of her muddy skirts and ragged cap, blushed, turned away hastily, brushed her clothes as well as she could with her hands, and went to find the girl with the pies.

'I hear you're looking for a scullery maid,' she said.

* * *

Gravity Sparrow had never worked in a kitchen before, but, confronted by a pile of dirty plates nearly as tall as she was, it wasn't hard to work out what to do.

There was a pump in the yard, so she could get clean water when she wanted it. You just had to keep a sharp lookout for carriages driven by reckless young men – which a lot of them were – and for the horses, which were everywhere. There were beautiful glossy hunters and small shaggy packhorses; comfortable hacks for round-bellied farmers; placid ladies' mares; and among them all the grooms and stable boys hurried, ducking under mighty heads and running backwards and forwards with bags of feed and bundles of hay. It wasn't till Gravity's third day, when she was getting used to all the busyness of the yard, that she heard someone calling the name of a small white-haired stable boy and realized that she knew him.

'*You're* Faithful Finch?' Gravity said, when they met at the pump. 'I knew you in the workhouse in Guildston. You were only a baby then.'

Gravity kept an eye out for Faithful from then on. He seemed to enjoy his work, and he was certainly good with the horses: even the most nervous animal would calm down when he took hold of its bridle.

It took Gravity two days to get to the bottom of the tottering pile of dirty dishes, and then it was time to embark on chopping the enormous numbers of onions that hung in plaits from the ceiling. She cried and cried over those onions, but once they were cooked they turned mysteriously sweet and delicious. Sitting on the kitchen doorstep, watching the comings and goings of the stable yard as she ate a pie, Gravity felt for a moment as rich as a princess.

It was on the fifth day of Gravity's new life that a smooth-faced gentleman rode into the yard. They were even busier that day than usual because Hannah the serving maid had been called away to nurse her mother, so Gravity took no particular notice of him until she heard his voice.

He only said, 'Take my horse', but the words sent a shiver down her spine.

Gravity peered cautiously out of the kitchen door. Yes, that was Sir William's steward, all right. Well, she'd polish his plate with the floor cloth if she got a chance.

She heard the steward's voice again later, when she was getting water from the pump. Through the window to the inn's private sitting room she saw the steward talking to Miss Spence, Sir William's sister.

'Yes,' said Cook, when Gravity mentioned it. 'He's got his eye on her for a wife.'

'Oh, but he's horrible!' protested Gravity.

The cook snorted.

'Yes, but he's a handsome gentleman for all that and has an uncle with money to leave. He's got a mind to marry into Sir William's family and get himself even richer than all his cheating and thieving have made him already.'

'But someone should tell Sir William about him!'

'I expect they already have, but Sir William's nothing but a noodle and he relies on the wretched steward too much to listen. Now, Gravity, that flummery pudding must be set by now, so off you go down to the cellar and bring it up here while I slice the lemons.'

The flummery was a sort of sweet solid porridge. It was made in small glasses, but Cook had poured the leftovers into a shallow bowl that wobbled like a full belly as Gravity carried it carefully up the cellar steps. She'd just got to the top when she heard the steward say, 'Quick with that horse, boy!' from the yard.

Gravity never wanted to see the steward again as long as she lived, so why she lingered to watch him she didn't know. But she did linger. She watched as Faithful ran up with a pretty grey mare, and she saw the steward, smirking, offer his hand to Miss Spence to lead her to the steps of the mounting block.

The fact that the mare stood on the steward's foot was entirely the steward's own fault for being in the way. In fact the whole thing would probably have passed off as an unfortunate accident if someone across the yard hadn't roared with laughter when the steward let out a yowl and began hopping about.

The steward flushed with fury, raised his riding whip and brought it down smartly across Faithful's shoulders.

Gravity wasn't sure exactly what happened next, but all of a sudden she found she was in the yard with the steward. Not only that, but the flummery bowl was empty in her hand, and white sticky stuff was dripping all down the steward's head and coat.

The steward raised his whip again, but a couple of packmen caught hold of him. After a few fierce efforts to free himself he stopped struggling, shook wild plumes of flummery from his hair, and stared at Gravity with burning, furious eyes.

'I'll see you never work in this town again,' he hissed. 'By the year's end you'll be begging in the gutter!'

Gravity went cold with dread – but then there was another laugh, and this time it came from the mounting block. The steward turned angrily, saw Miss Spence, and froze. Then he drew in a deep, steadying breath and even tried to laugh himself, though the sound came out as rusty and painful as the hinges on Mr Hodge's old door.

'My dear Miss Spence ... ' he began.

Miss Spence settled herself comfortably on her horse.

'I've heard many different stories about you,' she said to the steward, gathering up her reins, 'and I've never quite known what to believe. But I do now.'

The steward wiped a blob of flummery off his nose.

'Nothing you can tell him will damage Sir William's faith in me as his steward,' he said.

'No, but it has damaged mine in you as a man.' She smiled at Faithful and Gravity. 'Thank you for your service,' she said and trotted quickly away, leaving the steward dripping.

Faithful disappeared quickly, and Gravity dived hastily back into the kitchen. She was expecting a terrible scolding, but the cook was laughing so much she'd had to sit down.

'Oh don't fret,' said the cook at last. 'It was only a bit of leftover flummery. And it did me good to see it dripping down that man's smug face!'

As it turned out, Gravity was the heroine of the hour. Nearly everyone in town had come up against the steward at some point, and he was hated everywhere.

Unfortunately that didn't stop him being dangerous and powerful.

'He's a terrible man, but I can't afford to make an enemy of him,' the innkeeper explained, sadly. 'I'm sorry, child, but you can't work here any more.'

Gravity couldn't help but shed a tear or two as she made her way to the door of the King's Head for the last time. But as she did, a thin grey man looked up from his dinner, smiled and beckoned to her.

'I hear you're in need of a job,' he said, winking a bright brown eye.

Chapter 5
The Singing Sparrow

'But ... you haven't heard my voice,' said Gravity Sparrow, taken aback.

The thin man laughed.

'Not heard your voice! There's no one in this half of town hasn't heard your voice, Miss Sparrow. *How many pies do you want, Cook? Watch out, here comes the hot gravy! Faithful, can you bring Mr Brown's horse round?*'

Gravity blushed. She'd always been told off for being loud, but in the bustle of the King's Head she'd thought perhaps no one would notice her. If only she could be quiet and clean, with footsteps that pattered gently, like Miss Marianne ...

Her throat suddenly hurt at the thought of Miss Marianne and her old home. Most of the time Gravity managed to put the place out of her head, but sometimes she felt as if she were skating round the edge of a big whirlpool of sadness.

But there was no point in moping.

'Shouting's not the same as singing,' Gravity pointed out.

The grey man smiled.

'Oh, but it is,' he said. 'It's very much the same. If you have good lungs, then music must pour forth.'

Gravity felt extremely doubtful about this. She was willing to do any job, but selling song-sheets? Would anyone really buy song-sheets from her after they'd heard her bellowing out the songs in the street?

'I think you'll do well, for the story of that flummery will have got round and you'll be a heroine in the town,' the grey man explained. 'And as for me, I live in Guildston, and your steward can't reach me there. Won't you give it a try?'

Gravity took the bundle of song-sheets he offered. They had a picture of a little girl giving some flowers to a lady on them, but all the rest was a jumble of letters.

'I can't read,' she confessed. 'And I don't know the tune.'

'Well, I shall teach you,' said the grey man. 'Listen!' And he began to sing in such a sweet voice that Gravity quite forgot to listen to the words.

He laughed when she told him this and sang the song again. The words were quite easy to remember because most of them came along twice.

'Sing it with me this time,' he said. So she tried.

He was still smiling when they finished, though his smile had a slightly fixed look about it.

'Well, you have a good memory,' he said. 'But this time see if you can sing some of the same notes as me.'

*'Sweet cowslips I cry and ground ivy I sell
And round about London am known pretty well,
But when my sweet cowslips no longer abound
I cry my sweet cherries a penny a pound.
A penny a pound,
I cry my sweet cherries a penny a pound.'*

'Well, people will certainly hear you,' said the grey man, at last. 'Let's see how you get on this afternoon. I have business to attend to out of town, but meet me here when the clock strikes six, do you understand?'

Gravity had sometimes heard song-sheet sellers, and it had seemed a fine life to her. But she found it took some courage to walk out on to the quiet street and find a place to sing.

Gravity tried a place outside a baker's shop first, but no sooner had she cleared her throat than the baker sent his boy out to tell her to clear off before she frightened away his customers.

In the end she positioned herself outside a row of houses between the King's Head and a cobbler's. Everyone who came along the street would have to pass her.

'Sweet cowslips I cry and ground ivy I sell ... '

* * *

'Marianne! You're not attending to your sewing!' snapped Miss Dobbs.

Marianne jumped. There was a song-sheet seller bawling away somewhere outside in the street, and the sound had transported her miles away. Soon it would be Christmas, and by then Mama and Papa and Lawrence would be home. They'd been gone three whole months and Marianne wasn't sure she could remember laughing once since they'd left.

Marianne sighed and obediently cut off a length of thread. Mama had written to Mrs Bateman the housekeeper about the festivities, and the servants had been spurred into a bustle of baking and cleaning. That had made a nice change, because since Gravity Sparrow had left the house the servants had been nearly as scowling and cold as Miss Dobbs. It really wasn't *fair*: none of what had happened to Gravity had been Marianne's fault. Marianne hadn't done *anything*.

Marianne sighed again. When Lawrence heard about Gravity he was going to be very angry – and if he got to *see* Gravity he was going to be *furious*, because the sight of Gravity had given Marianne herself a horrible shock. Gravity had been a fine healthy girl when she'd left the house, but now she was pale and hollow-cheeked.

51

Gravity's clothes had shocked Marianne too. They were the ones she'd been wearing when she'd left the house, but now they were ragged and dirty.

Who would have thought that anyone could have changed so much in appearance in such a short time? And how could Gravity bear to wear that horrible old-lady hat?

Miss Dobbs got up and gave the schoolroom bell a vicious tug. Susannah had been getting slower and slower at answering the bell. Marianne suspected Susannah was doing it to be as annoying as possible, because all the servants had been doing as little for Miss Dobbs as they could. Why, Miss Dobbs's spider-fringed shawl, the one that had started off all the trouble with poor Gravity, hadn't even been washed yet. What's more, the servants hardly ever made Miss Dobbs what she ordered for dinner but, instead, something containing cheddar cheese, which gave her indigestion.

Miss Dobbs was glaring at Marianne as if Susannah's slowness was Marianne's fault.

'Where is that wretched girl?' Miss Dobbs snapped. 'I need her to order that dreadful song-sheet seller away. They shouldn't be allowed to disturb respectable people with their howling. I've a good mind to call for the constable!'

Miss Dobbs was always threatening to send for the constable.

The song-sheet seller's voice rose to a particularly ear-splitting squawk as she spoke, and Marianne suddenly realized something. That was Gravity Sparrow down there singing her head off!

'Susannah gets lazier and lazier,' went on Miss Dobbs, irritably. 'I shall recommend your dear mother dismisses her from her service.'

Miss Dobbs could recommend all she liked, but Mama wouldn't do any such thing. Marianne suddenly saw Miss Dobbs and Mama side by side in her mind. Miss Dobbs was always very correct, but ...

But sometimes, Marianne realized, you could be correct without being right. Why, Mama always made a point of buying a song-sheet or two from sellers just to be kind. Sometimes Mama would even tell them to call at the house for some food when they'd finished for the day. Mrs Bateman usually gave them some soup to help soothe their throats.

Marianne looked out of the window. It was getting dark, and the windows were rattling in their sashes. Where would Gravity sleep that night?

Outside, the singing rose to another painful screech. Marianne got up in a hurry.

'I'll see the song-sheet girl is told to go away, Miss Dobbs,' she said. 'I won't be long!' and she ran away before Miss Dobbs could lever open her scowling mouth to stop her.

Marianne ran to her bedroom, snatched her purse, ran down the stairs, pulled open the heavy front door and hurried down the six steps to street level.

She couldn't see Gravity, but Marianne could hear her defiantly light-hearted voice.

'I cry my sweet cherries a penny a pound.
A penny a pound,
I cry my sweet cherries a penny a pound.'

Marianne ran through the cruel December wind across the road and round the corner.

She was used to seeing the poor (that was what they were called – *the poor* – as if they were something quite separate from other people) but the sight of Gravity singing so bravely in the cold tore at her heart. People were hurrying past her, their heads down against the wind. What would happen if Gravity didn't sell any song-sheets? The thought was terrifying.

Marianne ran up to her.

'I want as many sheets as I can have for ten pence,' she said breathlessly. It was all she had left of the money Papa had given her before he'd left.

Gravity turned to her, beaming – and then her mouth fell open.

'Miss Marianne!' she exclaimed. She looked up and down the street. 'You're not out alone, Miss Marianne?'

Marianne couldn't believe that Gravity was giving a single thought to Marianne's own safety.

'I wanted to buy some song-sheets,' she said. 'I've got ten pence.'

Gravity still looked worried.

'But you'll only want one, Miss Marianne.'

'No,' said Marianne. 'No, I want more. There'll … there'll be parties at Christmas and people can have a copy each. It's such a pretty song.'

She held out her money and Gravity Sparrow clumsily counted out some song-sheets with hands that were red with cold.

'You'd better be getting back, Miss Marianne,' said Gravity.

Marianne wished she'd put on a coat so she could have given it to Gravity, but all she could do was say, 'Happy Christmas!' and run back round the corner and up the steps to the front door.

Whatever have we done? she asked herself in horror, as she closed the door behind her.

* * *

Gravity Sparrow was at the King's Head almost as soon as the clock struck six. She was very glad to get into the warm. She'd managed to sell some song-sheets, many of them to people who said, admiringly, 'You're the girl who threw the flummery over Sir William's steward, aren't you?'

Gravity searched all the public rooms, but she found no sign of the song-sheet man, and when she asked after him in the kitchen the cook shook her head sadly.

'It's that steward,' she said grimly. 'He's told your song-sheet man he'll be beaten up if he shows his face in town again. You're to leave the song-sheets with me, but your man says you can keep all the money you've earned, and good luck to you.'

Gravity gaped at the cook. It was cold, the wind was howling, and she had nowhere to stay.

'But ... what am I going to do?' she said.

Chapter 6
Night Soil Girl

The cook sighed.

'You'd be welcome to stay in my room, Gravity,' she said. 'But if that steward heard about it (and he would) then that'd mean I'd be out of a place too. You've made a powerful enemy there.'

'I seem to make them everywhere,' said Gravity, dolefully.

The cook hesitated.

'Look, let me find you something to eat,' she said. 'Things will look better when you've got something warm inside you.'

Gravity did feel better, but she still had no idea what to do. It looked as if she was going to have to get right out of town. Could she walk all the way to London with only a shilling and sixpence in her pocket?

London? thought Gravity. *How are you going to manage in London when you've made such a tangle of trying to earn a living here? What will the Londoners think of you, all covered in mud?*

Gravity washed up her bowl and spoon and crept out of the inn quietly when no one was looking. There were stars sparkling in the frosty sky and she sniffed the air of the stable yard. The last time she'd been here she'd thrown a bowlful of flummery over the steward's head. She grinned suddenly, because she found she still couldn't regret that one bit. She pulled her cloak tightly round her and set out across the dark yard.

She was approaching the gate when she heard a voice.

'Gravity!' someone whispered.

She looked round.

'Faithful?'

'Shh! Gravity, do you need somewhere to stay?'

'Yes, but no one in town will have me. So I'm off to seek my fortune!'

It sounded more hopeful when she put it like that.

'I think I know someone who'll have you,' whispered Faithful.

'Really? Who?'

Faithful gave Gravity directions.

'I'm almost sure she'll take you in,' he whispered. 'She was complaining just this morning that she can't keep hold of workers.'

Why not? wondered Gravity, but she thanked Faithful and, following his directions, made her way down the street and left down the alley beside the churchyard. It was pitch-black, and the cobbles were slippery with frost.

'Down to the bottom of the hill.' Gravity repeated Faithful's instructions to herself. 'But no further, or you'll end up in the canal.'

She went on cautiously, stumbling over wheel ruts and skidding on icy puddles. When a dog flung itself barking against the fence beside her, she recoiled so violently she nearly went head over heels.

The alley was pitch-dark, but across the roofs the yellow square of a high window shone out. It looked warm and safe. Gravity wondered if Master Lawrence was back from school yet and if Susannah was still cross about absolutely everything.

She went on until she hit her head on something, which was good because Faithful had said that when she hit her head on a sign by a doorway she'd have arrived.

Yes, here was a door. There was a light inside too.

Gravity took in a deep breath to give herself courage – and instantly regretted it. The place smelled absolutely disgusting. Still, beggars couldn't be choosers, she told herself. Gravity knocked on the door.

A curtain twitched and then a small window opened a crack.

'What do you want?' demanded a woman's voice.

'I'm looking for work, if you please, madam,' said Gravity.

The curtain was pulled aside to reveal a large shadowy shape.

'Aren't you the one who threw the pudding over the steward?' the voice demanded.

Gravity's heart sank.

'Yes, I am,' she admitted.

The woman nodded.

'A girl after my own heart,' she said. 'Well, you're too small really, but anyone who's thrown flummery over that steward is a friend of mine. I'll give you a trial.'

The door opened in front of Gravity and a strong, foul stench came out of it with the force of a stagecoach. It was so bad it pushed Gravity back several paces.

When Gravity had wiped her streaming eyes she saw that the woman at the door was a bulky person with a shrewd face and a steady eye.

'Well, don't just stand there,' the woman said. 'You'll let the cold in. Come in with you!'

* * *

Gravity was lucky, she knew that. The woman, whose name was Mrs Netty, gave Gravity shelter, food and an honest, useful employment. Gravity's new job not only kept the town free from rats and disease, but it was also the only position in town where the steward was never, ever going to notice her.

Mrs Netty was kind, too, under her abrupt manner. But …

But Gravity knew she would never have a friend again.

It was because of the terrible stink. It got into her clothes and her hair and there was no shifting it. Gravity soon lost the ability to detect it herself, but the frozen faces of the people she passed in the night-time streets told their own tale.

'Never you mind them,' Mrs Netty told her, briskly, as they got the cart ready for another night's work. 'All the night soil we collect has come from them, for all their face-pulling, and there's a fact. Now come and help me with the horse.'

The horse was old and wise and stopped all by himself at every door. Gravity and Mrs Netty would wheel their barrow up the path to the privy, tip out what was in the bucket and take it away.

Sometimes Mrs Netty would sniff deeply as she lifted out a bucket. 'Ooh, that'll clear your sinuses,' she'd say, with satisfaction. 'You won't catch a cold this winter, Gravity Sparrow, and that's a fact.'

And Mrs Netty was quite right, because Gravity smelled so horrible that no one was going to let her get near enough to give her a cold.

It was this that made Gravity realize how much she'd been looking forward to Master Lawrence coming home from school. Gravity had been almost sure she'd come across Master Lawrence somewhere: deep down, she'd been almost sure he'd seek her out.

But now he wouldn't want to be anywhere near her.

Hope withered within her.

Chapter 7
Presents from London

'Pay attention to your work, Marianne!' snapped Miss Dobbs. 'Some poor shivering child is waiting for you to finish that shirt!'

Marianne picked up her needle, but inside she was churning with anxious and rebellious thoughts. Miss Dobbs might pretend to care about the poor, but she didn't really, or she wouldn't have sent Gravity away. Marianne couldn't get Gravity out of her head. She'd looked so *cold*.

'Marianne!'

Marianne pushed her needle resentfully through the coarse cloth.

Lawrence was due back home that afternoon, and the thought of having to tell him about the stolen locket made it clear to Marianne that Miss Dobbs had been completely wrong about the whole thing. Why would Gravity have taken Miss Dobbs's locket? She couldn't wear it, and as for Miss Dobbs's silly ideas about her handing it to a criminal to sell for her ... Gravity didn't know any criminals! The only people Gravity knew were the people who lived in the house, and there were no criminals there. In fact, the person most like a criminal, Marianne now truly believed, was Miss Dobbs herself.

An urgent hammering sounded at the front door. It was the knock of someone who'd been away from home for months and was longing for fire and food and a warm welcome.

Marianne looked at Miss Dobbs. Downstairs, footsteps were hurrying across the hall to the front door.

'I think Lawrence is home,' said Marianne.

Now there were voices, and then boots clumping up the stairs, higher and higher, until the door burst open and Lawrence stormed in, cold and damp and smelling strange. He was taller too. Marianne found she was enormously happy to see him.

'Come on, Marianne,' said Lawrence, grabbing her hand. 'I've got a present for you. I've brought it all the way from London.'

Marianne was halfway down the stairs before she gave a thought to her sewing, or Miss Dobbs, left far behind above them – and then she didn't stop.

Lawrence threw open the lid of his trunk and burrowed inside. 'Here we are!' he said at last, triumphantly, as he scrambled to his feet and gave Marianne something. It was made of wood and was a bit like a cut-in-two ball with a very short stalk joining the two halves. 'It's a bandelore,' Lawrence told her, full of excitement. 'Look, there's a string wound round that stalk bit. You can make it spin right down to the bottom of the string and then back up again.' He took it back and showed her. It was marvellous, and after a few attempts Marianne found herself able to make it work too.

Lawrence had returned to rummaging in his trunk.

'Here's a cake for the servants,' he said, 'and here are some playing cards for Mama and Papa. And look, a boy's mother sent him some slippers, but the others made fun of them so I've brought them back to stop Gravity clattering about all the time.'

The bandelore ran to the end of its string, stopped, and began to spin unregarded.

Lawrence had stood up again, bursting with energy and joy.

'Come on, Marianne,' he said. 'Let's go downstairs and see if they fit her,' and he charged out of the room, bearing the servants' cake and the slippers.

Marianne, suddenly cold, hurried to follow him down the basement stairs.

* * *

Lawrence's cake was received with great delight.

'It won't be as good as one of yours,' he told Mrs Bateman, 'but it's a real London cake, so I thought you might be interested.'

'Well, *I* certainly am,' said Joseph, rubbing his hands gleefully. Even Susannah was smiling.

But then Lawrence said, 'Where's Gravity?' and all the Christmas jolliness fled away.

Lawrence looked from one to another of them.

'What's happened?' he demanded, suddenly anxious. 'She isn't ill? She's not –' He swallowed suddenly. 'She hasn't *died*?'

'No, no,' said Mrs Bateman hurriedly. 'No, I haven't heard but that she's well enough, Master Lawrence. But she's left the house. She's got a new position.'

Lawrence looked confused.

'But why would she do that?' he asked.

Everybody looked at one another, but no one said anything.

Lawrence turned to Marianne.

'Tell me,' he commanded. 'Tell me what happened.'

And Marianne burst into tears.

* * *

Marianne felt stupider and stupider as she told the story.

'What did you do then?' Lawrence kept asking: but the trouble was that Marianne hadn't done *anything*. She'd been quiet and good and let Miss Dobbs do as she pleased.

'But Gravity wouldn't steal a stupid locket!' exclaimed Lawrence.

'And so I told Miss Dobbs,' said Mrs Bateman. 'But it did no good. She said she couldn't risk keeping a thief in the house in case some of your mama's and papa's treasures went missing.'

Susannah snorted.

'Which was all just an excuse. She was in a rage over her shawl and her silly locket, that's all. She never had any reason to think Gravity had taken it.'

Marianne hadn't been able to bear the way Lawrence had kept asking her questions, and now she couldn't bear the fact that he'd stopped.

'We never found the locket,' she told him. 'Not that I think she took it,' she went on, quickly, 'but I searched and searched and I can't see where it could have gone.'

He waved this away.

'Never mind the locket,' he said. 'Gravity's the important thing. Does anyone know where she is?'

'She *was* working at the King's Head,' said Joseph. 'But she got the sack for throwing a bowl of flummery over Sir William's steward.'

Marianne gasped, but Lawrence punched the air.

'Hurrah for Gravity! When was that?'

'About a week ago, but I don't think anyone knows what's happened to her since then. She's quite disappeared.'

'She's a sturdy girl,' said Susannah, uneasily.

'Yes,' agreed Joseph. 'But that steward is a nasty piece of work.'

'Well then, we must go and find her,' said Lawrence.

He turned and ran back up the stairs past Marianne.

The front door closed with a bang in her face as Marianne went to follow him out of the hall into the street.

* * *

Lawrence came to Marianne's room later. He looked cold and tired.

'Did you find her?' asked Marianne, eagerly.

'I got news of her. She's working as a night soil collector.'

Marianne recoiled.

'What? How *could* she?' she said, in disgust.

'Well,' said Lawrence, drily, 'I should imagine it's better than starving.'

Marianne felt ashamed all over again.

'I should have tried to stop Miss Dobbs turning Gravity out of the house,' she said. 'I thought it was wrong to argue with her about it, but every time I've seen Gravity I've felt more and more how cruel it was to turn her away.'

Lawrence grunted.

'What do you think happened to the locket?' he asked.

'I don't know. I've been through the schoolroom again and again. I've even shaken all the books. The locket's not there, Lawrence. But no one could have gone into the schoolroom except one of the servants – and the servants were together the whole time, except for Gravity.'

'I suppose Miss Dobbs could have hidden it herself,' suggested Lawrence, 'so she had a reason for sending Gravity away.'

Marianne had wondered this herself, but she hadn't been able to get the idea to work.

'Miss Dobbs is mean and cruel,' she said. 'But the things she does are all very *good* mean and cruel things.'

'How can you have good mean things?'

'Well, like ... like telling yourself you're sending Gravity away to stop her stealing things from the house, even though it's really because you dislike her because she's loud and happy.'

'Oh, I see. Like the masters at school pretending that copying out proverbs is good for us, when it's really just to give them a chance for a doze,' suggested Lawrence.

Copying out proverbs had been the reason Marianne had been filling her inkwell on that terrible morning when Gravity had burst into the schoolroom.

'The servants all stood up for Gravity,' she said, thinking back.

'Even Susannah? She doesn't even really like her,' said Lawrence. 'Perhaps— '

'No. No. Gravity does annoy Susannah, but everything annoys Susannah. I think Susannah quite *likes* being annoyed. But it was Miss Dobbs that Susannah was angry with that day. She was *furious*.'

Marianne remembered Susannah balling up the fatal shawl and hurling it into the laundry basket with such force that Marianne had actually heard the thump as it landed.

Marianne gasped.

Susannah had hurled the shawl into the laundry basket …

'What's up?' asked Lawrence. 'You look like a goldfish.'

Marianne was frozen with sheer astonishment. *That* was what had happened!

She jumped up.

'Come on!' she said, and pulled open the door.

'Where?'

'To find the locket!' Marianne shouted, and she hurled herself down the moonlit stairs.

The laundry room was empty, but there was light enough to find candles and the tinderbox to light them.

The laundry basket had hardly been touched for weeks. It was almost impossible to get anything dry at this time of year, so underclothes were more or less the only things that were washed. Marianne opened the top of the basket and started pulling out mouldering items of clothing.

'Have you gone mad?' asked Lawrence, disentangling himself from a disgusting apron.

Marianne went deeper into the laundry basket.

'Bring that candle closer,' she said.

'Well, don't go and throw any more dirty clothes at me then, or you'll set me on fire.'

The smell at the bottom of the laundry basket was horrible, but ... yes! There was something shining smooth and pale in the candlelight. Miss Dobbs's shawl.

Marianne snatched it and shook it out, sending all the spider-legs kicking, and as she did, something went *tunk* against the side of the basket. Marianne ran her fingers through the fringe of the shawl until –

'Look!' she shouted, in triumph, and held up an oval disc surrounded by tiny pearls.

* * *

There was still a light under Miss Dobbs's door, but Lawrence and Marianne would probably have burst in anyway.

'I found it!' exclaimed Marianne, holding up the locket triumphantly.

'It must have got caught up on the fringe,' exclaimed Lawrence. 'Just think, it's been in the laundry basket all this time!'

Miss Dobbs took the locket, surveyed it coldly, and put it away carefully in her bag.

'I suppose the wretched child Sparrow must have hidden it in the basket and then never had the chance to retrieve it,' she said. 'If I had not expelled her at once from the house then no doubt it would have been whisked away.'

Lawrence gaped at her.

'But the locket was caught up on the fringe of your shawl,' he protested. 'Gravity wouldn't have gone anywhere near it!'

Miss Dobbs gave him a look that could make your insides feel as if they were full of cold maggots.

'It is not my habit to argue,' she said, coldly, 'but I will tell you this, Master Lawrence: while I live here, Gravity Sparrow shall never enter this house again!'

Chapter 8
Marianne's Choice

It was freezing the next morning and the sky was low and grey.

'I'm sure Mama and Papa will want Gravity back,' said Marianne to Lawrence at breakfast time. News had come that their parents would be home in time for dinner.

'I'm sure they will,' said Lawrence, gloomily. 'But you know how grown-ups stick together. They'll probably feel they have to believe Miss Dobbs, whatever we say.'

Susannah stopped on her way out of the room with the coal scuttle.

'I'm not sure the master and mistress will get here at all,' she said. 'That sky is full of snow. We might not see them for a week!'

Lawrence took a thoughtful bite of toast.

'We need to prove Gravity's not a thief.'

'But how can we do that? You can prove someone *is* a thief if you catch him climbing out of the window with your purse under his arm, but— '

Lawrence sat up.

'That's it!' he exclaimed. 'That's what we can do! When Gravity comes to collect the night soil tonight I'll let her see me climbing out of the window – only I'll be in disguise, of course – and then I'll drop something I've stolen from the house and run away. So then you scream, and once people come down to see what's the matter, Gravity can give back whatever it is I've stolen, and that will prove how honest she is! Yes, that's perfect. What could go wrong?'

More or less everything, thought Marianne, but Lawrence was alight with eagerness and there was no opportunity to say it.

'Hey, I know,' went on Lawrence, 'I'll steal one of the candlesticks from the dining room. They're really ugly.'

Marianne gulped. The candlesticks were certainly ugly, but they were old and valuable.

She tried her best to think of a better way to prove Gravity's innocence. But she couldn't.

Things were happening much too fast.

* * *

Outside in the evening light the snow had begun to swirl down. Marianne hoped that Mama and Papa were nearly home. Miss Dobbs had been fussing around all day making sure everything was clean and tidy, and Marianne had hardly had a minute to think properly about Lawrence's plan.

'I don't know how to scream,' she whispered, as she passed him on the stairs.

'Well, shout "Help, help! Burglars!" then,' said Lawrence, exasperated. Then he looked round sharply as wheels sounded outside. 'Hey, Marianne, listen! Yes, it's a *carriage*!'

From then on there was no time even for worrying, for here were Mama and Papa, smiling and ducking hastily into the house to avoid the blizzard – and here were two more grown-ups as well.

'Sir William, Miss Spence, you know my children,' said Papa, brushing snow off his coat on to the newly polished floor. 'Ah, Joseph, good to see you. There's a fire in the drawing room?'

'Yes, sir,' said Joseph, collecting coats.

'Come then, Sir William. Come, Miss Spence. Come and get warm.'

'We came across Sir William's carriage stuck in a drift of snow, so we have offered Sir William and Miss Spence shelter for the night,' Mama told Joseph, apologetically. 'Perhaps you would tell Mrs Bateman and have Susannah and Gravity make up fires in the guest rooms. The snow's amazingly deep a mile out of town. Ah, Miss Dobbs! How nicely you have kept the house. No, no, Miss Dobbs, keep your report for tomorrow when we can go through it all comfortably. Oh, how good it is to be home!'

Dinner was a very noisy affair, with Mama talking about the factories in the north, Sir William complaining fretfully about how badly his estate was doing, and Lawrence answering Papa's questions about school. Marianne tried to enjoy it, but Lawrence's plan to help Gravity was very worrying.

'Dear Marianne, I have missed you,' whispered Mama, when Marianne said goodnight. 'Tomorrow we shall have a nice cosy time together, but with Sir William and Miss Spence here there is no time now.'

Lawrence caught Marianne on her way to her room.

'I'll come to your room when Mama and Papa have gone to bed,' he said in a low voice. 'Then we'll go downstairs and wait for the night soil cart.'

* * *

Marianne had wrapped herself in a shawl and put on her slippers, for the house was freezing, and once Lawrence had opened the dining room window so they'd hear the night soil cart arriving, it was even worse. He'd opened the parlour window too, so he could get back into the house again unobserved. Marianne didn't know whether her teeth were chattering more with cold or nerves. She was wondering if there was any chance the snow would stop the night soil cart coming when Lawrence said, 'Shh!'

There was a creaking outside, of heavy wheels on snow.

'That's the cart,' whispered Lawrence, adjusting the scarf he'd tied round his face. He'd 'borrowed' Joseph's old ratting hat, and what Marianne could see of Lawrence in the silver streaks of moonlight that came through the gaps in the curtains looked sinister and most unlike himself.

'Right,' said Lawrence, 'hand me that candlestick and then go and hide behind the curtain. When you hear me shout, count to ten and then scream.'

Marianne had a hundred objections to this, but Lawrence was already tucking a candlestick under his arm, sliding the window further up and poking out his head.

The plan was that Lawrence and Gravity would come face to face on the path outside the window, but things went wrong even quicker than Marianne had imagined. Lawrence was only halfway out of the window when someone appeared on the path outside and grabbed his arm.

Lawrence squawked and recoiled, but the grip on his arm was amazingly strong and all he managed to do was drag the person into the room with him. There were a few confused moments of struggling, and then someone bellowed: 'Help! Help! Burglars!'

This saved Marianne the trouble of screaming, of course, but she found herself screaming anyway, because that wasn't Gravity Sparrow's voice – that was someone much older!

Then Marianne got a glimpse of a beefy arm wielding the candlestick like a club and she screamed again. She rushed over to try to help Lawrence, but it was so dark she could hardly tell who she was thumping. Now someone else was climbing in over the sill. Marianne, in a panic, got hold of something she thought she recognized as Lawrence's sleeve and by giving it a tremendous heave she managed to break him away from his assailant just in time to dodge a heavy blow from the candlestick.

There was a roar of frustration and then another impact followed by a squeak of pain. Various people fell over each other and just for an instant Marianne saw the window opening, clear save for the swirling snow.

'Quick!' whispered Marianne. 'Get out!'

Lawrence dived for the window, scrambled out and was gone.

'Get off me!' bellowed someone on the black floor in front of her. 'Get off me, you great hummock!'

'Mrs Netty?' asked an uncertain voice which certainly belonged to Gravity Sparrow. 'I thought you were a burglar!'

'Do I *smell* like a burglar? Get off me!'

Marianne stood, gasping. This was partly from fear, and partly so she wouldn't have to smell Mrs Netty and Gravity. She was realizing to her dismay that there were people moving above her head – she could hear sharp questions, and feet coming down the stairs. Marianne retreated behind the curtains again, and so when Papa came in carrying a candle and a stout stick he saw only Mrs Netty, clutching a candlestick, and Gravity Sparrow.

'What's going on?' he asked, reasonably enough. 'What are you doing with that candlestick?'

'Clobbering a thieving villain,' answered Mrs Netty, doughtily, from the floor.

'But he got away, sir,' volunteered Gravity. 'I got his shoe though!' and she held one up.

There was the rustling of skirts in the hall and Mama and Miss Dobbs and Miss Spence came in with candles. And there, in a purple nightcap, was Sir William, blinking round nervously and asking what the matter was. Then all the servants began arriving, and in the confusion Marianne got the chance to slip out from behind the curtain unnoticed.

Lawrence was one of the last to come in. He gave Marianne a rather tremulous smile.

'Whatever's happened?' asked Miss Spence.

'I'm not sure yet, my dear,' said Mama, comfortably. 'But I believe I heard someone call "thief".'

Miss Dobbs spoke, bony and scowling and, oddly, fully dressed.

'*Two* thieves!' she proclaimed. 'Just as I thought. I always stay up waiting for the night soil men, madam, for fear they might attempt a trick like this. And there's Gravity Sparrow, whom I expelled from the house some months ago for stealing, back at her old game!'

'I didn't steal anything!' squeaked Gravity.

'Oh, but surely—' began Mama.

'And the child clearly has an accomplice,' went on Miss Dobbs, drawing back in distaste from the large and stinking stranger by the window. 'Led by Sparrow to the place where she knew the valuables were to be found!'

Mama looked at Papa.

'I'm sure Gravity couldn't have meant any harm,' she said.

Sir William pulled worriedly at his chin.

'This is a very serious matter,' he said. 'These night soil people have the perfect opportunity to rob houses. They must be arrested.'

Marianne gasped. You could be hanged for stealing. Miss Dobbs gave a cold smile.

'I am ready to give evidence, Sir William, unpleasant a duty though it is,' she said.

Mrs Netty heaved herself up from the floor. The movement stirred up a powerful pong, and all the ladies clasped handkerchiefs to their noses.

'Thief?' demanded Mrs Netty, outraged. 'I'm no thief – I'm a respectable woman, I am, with a respectable trade. I saw some villain coming out of your window and collared him, but he dragged me inside.'

'And I heard the racket and came to help,' said Gravity, anxiously. 'Only,' she went on, her face falling, 'I don't think I *did* help much, because in the dark everything got muddled up and he got away.'

'How convenient,' said Miss Dobbs, coldly. 'And now the villain has gone off into the snow, I suppose. No doubt if you hadn't been disturbed then the candlestick would have gone with him.'

Lawrence took a deep breath.

'No,' he said. 'It wouldn't have done. You see – ' He swallowed, hard. 'You see, I was the thief.'

'What?' said Papa.

'I can prove it too,' said Lawrence. 'That shoe Gravity's got. Look, it's the same as this one I'm wearing.'

Papa took both shoes and compared them.

'They look the same to me,' he said. 'Lawrence, what were you doing climbing out of the window? Wouldn't a door have been easier? And if you *must* steal candlesticks, couldn't you have taken a less valuable one?'

It took a while to explain.

'Nonsense!' said Miss Dobbs, when Lawrence had finished. 'The boy has made this tale up to save the child Sparrow.'

'That's quite possible,' said Sir William, worriedly. 'We must have these people arrested until we can get to the truth of this matter.'

'My dear,' said Mama to Papa, 'first of all, do give Lawrence his shoes back. He'll be getting cold, running about in his bare feet.'

'Oh!' said Marianne. Everyone turned to look at her, but a great warm idea had swept over her and she hardly noticed. 'Mama!' she went on. 'If we look at the marks in the snow then we will be able to see if Lawrence is telling the truth, because then there'll be tracks of a bare foot running round the house and back inside again!'

Everybody was quite excited by this idea, and Papa and Joseph went outside with lanterns, despite all the ladies' protests about chills, and inspected the tracks in the snow. They came back shivering, but rather pleased with themselves.

'Marianne has entirely proved your innocence, madam,' Papa told Mrs Netty, politely. 'The bare-footed thief ran round the house and back in again at the parlour window.'

'Does that prove my innocence too?' asked Gravity, anxiously.

'Yours too, Gravity,' said Mama.

'Indeed,' said Sir William to Gravity, 'you must be a very brave girl. In fact I think I've seen you before. Yes, you were the girl living with old Mr and Mrs Hodge. Are they comfortably settled into their new house?'

So then Gravity told Sir William all about the steward setting fire to the cottage and not giving the Hodges the money they were due for their cow and their land.

Sir William was horrified.

'But I've trusted my steward completely,' he said. 'Why, I've been encouraging him to marry my sister! Can he really have been stealing the money I've given him to pay people?'

'He's been doing worse than that,' said Mrs Netty, grimly, and told him all about the steward's wicked ways in the town. 'That's the only reason I employed Gravity,' she told him. 'I need someone with the strength of an adult, really, but no one would give the poor girl a daylight job for fear of the steward, and she was likely to starve else.'

'There, brother,' said Miss Spence. 'The wretched steward is dishonest, as well as ill-tempered. No wonder the estate has been doing badly if he has been stealing your money. You won't want him to marry me now, will you?'

'No indeed,' said Sir William. 'And he'll not be able to marry anyone, for as soon as I am home I shall have him tied hand and foot and thrown into gaol.'

'And I shall write to his rich old uncle, to tell him all about it,' said Miss Spence, happily. 'And then I'm sure he'll want to find a more deserving place to leave his money.'

Mama smiled round at everyone.

'So Gravity Sparrow is the heroine of the hour,' she said.

'Together with the excellent Mrs Netty,' said Papa. 'Mrs Netty, I think we must take Gravity off your hands so you'll be able to hire a larger assistant. Quite honestly, even with Gravity living among us, the house can only be quieter than this.'

'And Miss Dobbs must say sorry to Gravity,' said Lawrence.

Everyone turned expectantly to Miss Dobbs.

'Say sorry?' Miss Dobbs echoed, recoiling as if someone had thrust a dead rat under her nose. 'Me? Apologize to some grubby child of the gutter?'

'Well,' said Sir William, 'the girl does seem to have been treated rather unfairly.'

'Yes,' said Miss Spence. 'It should be done.'

Miss Dobbs was suddenly trembling with rage. 'I have *never* been so insulted!' she said. 'Never. To think of me, the sister of a judge, expected to demean myself in this way. It cannot be borne. I shall leave the house at once!'

Mama blinked.

'But dear Miss Dobbs, it is the middle of the night. There is snow on the ground—'

'No matter. I shall hire a horse to take me to my brother the judge's house. Have my things sent there, if you please. And now I bid you all goodbye!'

Miss Dobbs marched from the room and across the hall. Everyone stood, too surprised to speak, as the front door opened and slammed. Almost immediately there was a loud clattering sound and a sharp howl of dismay.

Mrs Netty shook her head.

'You left the night soil bucket on the path again, didn't you?' she said accusingly to Gravity.

Gravity clapped a hand to her mouth in horror.

'I just dropped everything when I heard you shouting for help,' she said. 'Oh dear, Miss Dobbs will have got the stuff all over her!'

Even Mama couldn't look very concerned.

Papa rubbed his hands together. 'Well, this seems to have been a very good night's work,' he said.

'Except that Marianne has lost her governess,' said Mama ruefully. 'Oh dear, it's going to be such a bother finding a new one.'

'Not if you send Marianne to school,' said Lawrence.

Marianne jumped at the thought. *School? Being with lots of other girls, instead of being stuck upstairs with someone like Miss Dobbs all the time?*

Mama looked doubtful.

'But Marianne is such a quiet, shy little thing,' she said. 'Surely she'd be miserable at school.'

Lawrence put an arm round Marianne's shoulders.

'Marianne wasn't too shy to help Gravity,' he said.

'And Marianne was the one who worked out how to prove Gravity's innocence,' pointed out Papa.

'*And* she found the locket,' said Lawrence.

'Really?' said Papa. 'Then I think Marianne's mind deserves to be carefully trained.'

Mama looked at Marianne.

'Well,' she said. 'Would you like to go away to school?'

Marianne was filled with horror and fear and longing and curiosity, all at once. She opened her mouth without knowing what it was she was going to say.

'Yes,' she said at last. 'Yes, Mama! Yes! I'd *love* to go to school!'

School in the time of *Hand and Foot*

At the end of the story, Marianne can't wait to go to school – but what would school have been like when she got there?

This story is set in England in the 1790s, when King George III was on the throne and it was very fashionable to wear a big white curly wig. In those days, not all children went to school – and those who did go would have had very different experiences from each other, depending on whether they were a boy or a girl, or rich or poor.

Lawrence and the boarding school

In the eighteenth century, most schools were just for boys – no girls allowed. The most important subject at these schools was learning to write and speak in Latin. Boys would also be taught grammar, Ancient Greek, and how to write a letter – and, if they were lucky, some music, science, maths, geography, French and Italian. The lessons weren't very interesting though: the boys spent most of their time copying things down or learning sets of Latin words which they had to recite by heart.

Many boys went to grammar schools, where Latin and Ancient Greek took up most of the lessons. Lawrence's parents wanted to make sure he learned some maths too, so they paid for him to go to a private boarding school in London. He stayed at school for the whole term, sleeping in a dormitory and eating his meals there too – the food wasn't very nice! His teachers, who were called the 'masters', were very interested in the money that his parents paid for the school and not at all interested in getting Lawrence to learn anything – but he enjoyed himself all the same.

Marianne and her governess

While boys went off to school, it was much more common for girls to stay at home and be taught by a governess. A governess was like a teacher who lived in your house. Miss Dobbs taught Marianne reading, writing and arithmetic, as well as some French, geography, sewing, and learning all the Roman emperors and the kings of England off by heart.

But lots of other girls wouldn't have been taught half as much as Marianne was by Miss Dobbs. Instead, they learned some drawing, dancing, music, embroidery and maybe a little bit of French. Lots of people thought that girls just needed talents to attract a husband and didn't need to know anything else. While the sons from wealthy families were supposed to go to university, travel around Europe seeing the sights on a 'grand tour' and then perhaps take up a profession, the daughters were only supposed to get married and then look after the house and children.

Although Miss Dobbs taught Marianne a lot, she was very strict and uncompromising. Marianne often felt lonely in her long lessons, and so she was very excited when she was allowed to go to school and do her lessons with other girls her age.

Gravity and the workhouse school

Lawrence and Marianne's parents were quite wealthy and could afford to pay for governesses or schools, but things were quite different for poorer children like Gravity.

When Gravity met Faithful Finch at the King's Head, she remembered him from the workhouse where they grew up. Workhouses were buildings where people who had no homes or money went to live. There they would be fed and clothed but would have to do tiring jobs all day, like breaking stones or washing laundry. Some of the workhouses were horrible, unclean places to live, but the one Gravity grew up in wasn't as bad as those.

The children who lived in the workhouses might have spent a few hours per day in a sort of school, but they didn't get to learn anything very interesting. Often they were only taught the skills that would be useful to them when they got jobs as maids or labourers. Some people even thought that it was dangerous to teach writing and maths to poor children, in case they got too clever and started complaining about being servants! Gravity learned how to sew and say her prayers at her workhouse school, but not how to read.

Gravity and Faithful grew up in the workhouse because they had lost their parents and had no one to look after them. That is why they both have unusual names. The people who ran the workhouse didn't want to keep thinking of new names every time a new baby arrived, so they used a system: the first name would be a good quality that they hoped the child would have, and the surname would be a bird. The people who named Gravity hoped she would be a careful and serious person – of course she turned out to be quite the opposite, although still wonderful in her own way!